Congressional
Research
Service

Federal Benefits and the Same-Sex Partners of Federal Employees

Wendy Ginsberg
Analyst in American National Government

John J. Topoleski
Analyst in Income Security

December 21, 2012

Congressional Research Service

7-5700

www.crs.gov

R42873

Summary

The federal government provides a variety of benefits to its 4.4 million civilian and military employees and 4.7 million civilian and military retirees. Among these benefits are health insurance; enhanced dental and vision benefits; survivor benefits; retirement and disability benefits; family, medical, and emergency leave; and reimbursement of relocation costs. Pursuant to Title 5 U.S.C. Chapters 89, 89A, 89B, and other statutes, federal employees may extend these benefits to eligible spouses and children.

In 1996, Congress passed the Defense of Marriage Act (DOMA, P.L. 104-199; 1 U.S.C §7) "[t]o define and protect the institution of marriage." DOMA contains two provisions. The first provision allows all states, territories, possessions, and Indian tribes to refuse to recognize an act of any other jurisdiction that designates a relationship between individuals of the same sex as a marriage. The second provision prohibits federal recognition of these unions for purposes of federal enactments. Pursuant to DOMA, the same-sex partners of federal employees are not eligible to receive federal benefits that are extended to the spouses of federal employees. An estimated 34,000 federal employees are in same-sex relationships—including state-recognized marriages, civil unions, or domestic partnerships.

The Obama Administration has extended certain benefits to the same-sex partners of federal employees and annuitants—and argued that it has done so within the parameters of existing federal statutes. On June 2, 2010, President Obama released a memorandum that extended specific benefits to the same-sex partners of federal employees, including coverage of travel, relocation, and subsistence payments.

Some Members of Congress argue that same-sex partners of federal employees should have access to benefits afforded married, opposite-sex couples in order to attract the most efficient and effective employees to federal service. Other Members of Congress argue that the law prohibits the extension of such benefits, and, therefore, actions to distribute any spousal benefits to same-sex couples is contrary to both the text and spirit of DOMA.

Congress has had a long-standing interest in overseeing the benefits provided to federal employees. On the one hand, the federal government seeks to attract the most effective, highly trained workforce to address technical and complex issues. On the other hand, finite resources can present challenges when considering whether to extend benefits to federal employees. When DOMA was enacted, the House report that accompanied the legislation stated that a primary goal of the law was to "preserve scarce government resources."

The Congressional Budget Office (CBO) estimated that extending benefits to the partners of employees in same-sex relationships pursuant to S. 1910 would cost the federal government $144 million in discretionary spending between 2013 and 2022. CBO also estimated, however, that extending the benefits could "limit future rate increases" in federal health care costs because health care providers would be required to recover certain health care costs that previously went unrecovered. These recovered costs could lower the federal government's health care premiums.

In the 112th Congress, two bills have been introduced that, if enacted, would permit federal employees to extend insurance, long-term care, and other benefits to same-sex partners. On November 18, 2011, Senator Joseph Lieberman introduced S. 1910, the Domestic Partnership Benefits and Obligations Act of 2011. That same day, Representative Tammy Baldwin introduced a companion bill, H.R. 3485, also called the Domestic Partnership Benefits and Obligations Act of 2011, in the House. On May 16, 2012, S. 1910 was ordered to be reported favorably from the Committee on Homeland Security and Governmental Affairs. H.R. 3485 was referred to multiple committees, but no further action has been taken on the bill.

This report examines current policies on the application of benefits to the same-sex partners of federal employees and reviews certain policy debates about the extension or removal of these benefits. This report also presents data on the prevalence of same-sex partner benefits in the private and public sector. This report focuses on federal benefits for same-sex partners and not on same-sex relationships in general. For more information on the implementation of DOMA and how it affects same-sex partnerships, see CRS Report RL31994, *Same-Sex Marriages: Legal Issues*, by Alison M. Smith. For information on private sector employee benefit plans and same-sex partner benefits, see CRS Report R41998, *Same-Sex Marriage and Employee Benefit Plans: Legal Considerations*, by Jennifer Staman.

Contents

Tables

Contacts

Introduction

In 1996, Congress passed the Defense of Marriage Act (DOMA, P.L. 104-199) "[t]o define and protect the institution of marriage."[1] DOMA (1) allows states to refuse to recognize same-sex marriages or partnerships and (2) limits the recognition of these same-sex partnerships for purposes of any act of Congress or by any federal bureau or agency.[2] As codified, DOMA has three sections. The first provides the bill's name, the second section allows states to determine whether to recognize same-sex marriage, and the third defines the terms *marriage* and *spouse* for the purposes of federal enactments. Specifically, Section 3 of DOMA says the following:

> In determining the meaning of any Act of Congress, or of any ruling, regulation, or interpretation of the various administrative bureaus and agencies of the United States, the word "marriage" means only a legal union between one man and one woman as husband and wife, and the word "spouse" refers only to a person of the opposite sex who is a husband or a wife.[3]

The federal government provides a variety of benefits to its workforce, including health care, life insurance, pensions, and paid time off for vacation and sick leave. Federal employees are permitted by law to extend certain health, long-term care, and other benefits to their spouses. DOMA prohibits the distribution of these spousal benefits to same-sex partners. The federal government, however, provides other benefits to federal employees that may be extended to those who are associated with a federal employee, but who are not necessarily the employee's spouse. In some cases, these benefits have been extended to the partners of federal employees who are in same-sex relationships.

On June 17, 2009, President Obama issued a memorandum directing executive agencies to examine ways to extend benefits to federal employees in same-sex domestic partnerships or same-sex marriages[4] within the authority of existing law.[5] On July 10, 2009, Office of Personnel

---

[1] 1 U.S.C §7.

[2] For more information on DOMA and its effects on same-sex marriages, see CRS Report RL31994, *Same-Sex Marriages: Legal Issues*, by Alison M. Smith.

[3] 1 U.S.C. §7.

[4] Although there is a legal distinction between same-sex partners and same-sex marriages, this report refers to both institutions as same-sex partnerships. In this report, the term "same-sex partnership" includes a legal marriage, same-sex partners who chose not to get married, and partners who have been unable to get married for any reason. OPM regulations define a domestic partnership as a committed relationship of two adults of the same-sex, in which the partners

> (1) are each other's sole domestic partner and intend to remain so indefinitely; (2) maintain a common residence, and intend to continue to do so (or would maintain a common residence but for an assignment abroad or other employment-related, financial, or similar obstacle); (3) are at least 18 years of age and mentally competent to consent to contract; (4) share responsibility for a significant measure of each other's financial obligations; (5) are not married or joined in a civil union to anyone else; (6) are not the domestic partner of anyone else; (7) are not related in a way that, if they were of opposite sex, would prohibit legal marriage in the U.S. jurisdiction in which the partnership was formed; (8) are willing to certify, if required by the agency, that they understand that willful falsification of any documentation required to establish that an individual is in a domestic partnership may lead to disciplinary action and the recovery of the cost of benefits received related to such falsification, as well as constitute a criminal violation under 18 U.S.C. § 1001, and that the method for securing such certification, if required, shall be determined by the agency; and (9) are willing promptly to disclose, if required by the agency, any dissolution or

(continued...)

Management (OPM) Director John Berry issued a memorandum directing all executive-branch agencies to review and report on the benefits offered to opposite-sex partners—whether married or not—of federal employees.[6] OPM and the Department of Justice (DOJ) reviewed these reports and suggested to President Obama actions that would extend some benefits to the same-sex partners of federal employees.

On June 2, 2010, President Obama released a second memorandum that extended specific benefits and perquisites to the same-sex partners of federal employees. For certain benefits, the term *spouse* is either not found in the benefit's authorizing language or the authorizing language widens the scope of eligibility. The benefits that were extended by the memorandum are those whose authorizing statutes do not use the term *spouse* to define or limit potential recipients of the benefit. The Administration argues that its actions comply with all federal laws, including DOMA. Among other benefits, the memorandum extended certain childcare and sick leave benefits that had previously only been available to opposite-sex spouses—including the authority to take up to 24 hours of unpaid leave when a same-sex partner or a partner's child is ill. The newly extended benefits were made available upon the second memorandum's release.

In the 112th Congress, two bills have been introduced that, if enacted, would permit a federal employee to provide insurance, travel, and other benefits to his or her same-sex partner. On November 18, 2011, Senator Joseph Lieberman introduced S. 1910, the Domestic Partnership Benefits and Obligations Act of 2011, and Representative Tammy Baldwin introduced a companion bill, H.R. 3485.[7] On May 16, 2012, S. 1910 was ordered to be reported favorably from the Committee on Homeland Security and Governmental Affairs. H.R. 3485 was referred to the House Oversight and Government Reform Committee's Subcommittee on Workforce Protections, the House Education and the Workforce's Subcommittee on Workforce Protections, the House Judiciary's Subcommittee on Courts, Commercial and Administrative Law, and the Committee on House Administration. No further action has been taken on the bill.

(...continued)

material change in the status of the domestic partnership.

Generally, apart from same-sex marriages, the federal government recognizes marriages that are valid in a state. For example, according to a telephone conversation between the authors and an OPM official on November 18, 2009, federal employees who are in opposite-sex common-law marriages qualify for federal benefits. This information was again verified by OPM via e-mail to the authors on November 1, 2012. Common-law marriages, which are recognized in nine states and the District of Columbia (and are restricted by date in five additional states), are defined differently in each state. Generally, however, such a marriage requires a couple to live together for an unspecified but considerable length of time, and to generally understand themselves to operate as a married couple, despite not having a marriage license or other government-sanctioned document. In addition, most states will generally recognize a common-law marriage validly entered into in another state, even if the couple could not enter into a valid common-law marriage in that state.

[5] U.S. President (Obama), "Memorandum for the Heads of Executive Departments and Agencies, Subject: Federal Benefits and Non-discrimination," June 17, 2009, at http://www.whitehouse.gov/the_press_office/Memorandum-for-the-Heads-of-Executive-Departments-and-Agencies-on-Federal-Benefits-and-Non-Discrimination-6-17-09/. Among the benefits that could be extended are relocation and travel expenses for same-sex domestic partners.

[6] John Berry, *Memorandum for Heads of Executive Departments and Agencies*, Office of Personnel Management, Subject: Federal Benefits for Same-Sex Domestic Partners, July 10, 2009, at http://www.chcoc.gov/Transmittals/TransmittalDetails.aspx?TransmittalId=2384.

[7] S. 1910 would extend same-sex partner benefits to the following federal employees: those as defined in 5 U.S.C. §§2105, 8331, 8401, 8701, 8901, or 9001; Members of Congress; the President; any other employee who is included in regulations that would be promulgated by OPM. H.R. 3485 includes similar, but not identical, language.

Congress may elect to examine, prohibit, or codify Administration initiatives that made some benefits available to same-sex partners. Congress has the authority to determine if some, all, or none of the benefits that are available to the opposite-sex spouses of federal employees should be made available to the same-sex partners of federal employees.

The Defense of Marriage Act and Federal Benefits

The federal government provides a variety of benefits to federal civilian and military employees and retirees.[8] Among these benefits are health insurance; enhanced dental and vision benefits; retirement and disability benefits and plans; survivor benefits; family, medical, and emergency leave; and reimbursement of relocation costs. Various federal laws and regulations determine who is eligible to receive these benefits. A federal employee who is married to someone of the opposite gender can, pursuant to federal law, extend many of these benefits to his or her spouse.

DOMA[9] affects the application of benefits to the spouses and partners of federal employees.[10] DOMA defines *marriage* explicitly as "only a legal union between one man and one woman as husband and wife."[11] DOMA defines *spouse* as "a person of the opposite sex who is a husband or a wife."[12] Pursuant to DOMA, these definitions are to be used when "determining the meaning of any Act of Congress."[13] As such, DOMA prohibits the extension of any federal spousal benefit to the same-sex partners of federal employees.[14] In addition, specific laws or regulations, like the regulations for the Family Medical Leave Act, explicitly define spouse as a member of the opposite sex.

Report language from the House Committee on the Judiciary in support of H.R. 3396 (104th Congress; later enacted as DOMA) stated in its introduction that DOMA sought to protect states' rights to determine whether same-sex couples could marry and be eligible for benefits. DOMA, the report argued, anticipated certain legal questions that could arise from this arrangement. The report said the following:

---

[8] In 2010, there were 2.8 million active federal civilian employees (including U.S. Postal Service), 1.6 million military employees, 1.9 million civilian annuitants (non-U.S. Postal Service), 580,000 U.S. Postal Service annuitants, and 2.3 million military retirees. The number of federal civilian and military employees is available from OPM's "Historical Federal Workforce Tables," at http://www.opm.gov/feddata/HistoricalTables/TotalGovernmentSince1962.asp. The number of federal civilian annuitants is from OPM's, *Statistical Abstracts Fiscal Year 2011: Federal Employee Benefits Programs*, p. 9, at http://www.fedbens.us/Retire_Stats.pdf. The number of U.S. Postal Service annuitants is from OPM's *FY2011 Civil Service Retirement and Disability Fund Annual Report*, January 2012, p. 12. The number of military retirees is from the Department of Defense, *2010 Demographics Report: Profiles of the Military Community*, at http://www.militaryhomefront.dod.mil/12038/Project%20Documents/MilitaryHOMEFRONT/Reports/2010_Demographics_Report.pdf.

[9] 1 U.S.C. §7.

[10] The unmarried partner of a federal employee of the opposite gender would also not be eligible for these benefits. This report, however, focuses on eligibility of same-sex domestic partners.

[11] 1 U.S.C. §7.

[12] Ibid.

[13] Several federal courts have ruled on the constitutionality of Section 3 of DOMA, and the Supreme Court has agreed to rule on the issue during the current term. The Department of Justice indicated that it would not defend the constitutionality of DOMA, although the Administration said that it would continue to enforce the law. The Speaker of the House of Representatives convened the Bipartisan Legal Advisory Group to defend DOMA in the federal courts. For more information on DOMA, see CRS Report RL31994, *Same-Sex Marriages: Legal Issues*, by Alison M. Smith.

[14] Several federal employees are challenging the constitutionality of DOMA's prohibition of benefits to their partners.

> With regard to federal law, a decision by one State to authorize same-sex "marriage" would raise the issue of whether such couples are entitled to federal benefits that depend on marital status. H.R. 3396 anticipates these complicated questions by laying down clear rules to guide their resolution, and it does so in a manner that preserves each State's ability to decide the underlying policy issue however it chooses.[15]

According to report language, the federal government had four specific interests in mind when drafting DOMA:

- defending and nurturing the institution of traditional, heterosexual marriage;

- defending traditional notions of morality;

- protecting state sovereignty and democratic self-governance; and

- preserving scarce government resources.[16]

The latter governmental interest was described in greater detail later in the report:

> Government currently provides an array of material and other benefits to married couples in an effort to promote, protect, and prefer the institution of marriage. While the Committee has not undertaken an exhaustive examination of those benefits, it is clear that they do impose certain fiscal obligations on the federal government. For example, survivorship benefits paid to the surviving spouse of a veteran of the Armed Services plainly cost the federal government money.

> If Hawaii (or some other State) were to permit homosexuals to "marry," these marital benefits would, absent some legislative response, presumably have to be made available to homosexual couples and surviving spouses of homosexual "marriages" on the same terms as they are now available to opposite-sex married couples and spouses. To deny federal recognition to same-sex "marriages" will thus preserve scarce government resources, surely a legitimate government purpose.[17]

Executive Branch Actions to Extend Benefits to Same-Sex Partners of Federal Employees

Some benefits to federal employees are extended specifically to the spouse of the federal employee, while the laws and regulations governing other benefits may not explicitly use the term spouse. The Obama Administration has extended to the same-sex partners of federal employees some benefits that do not have the term spouse in their governing authorities. The Administration has argued that they have done so within the parameters of DOMA. Some organizations, however, including the non-profit Family Research Council, have argued that the extension of these benefits is both costly and could undermine the federal definition of marriage.[18]

---

[15] U.S. Congress, House Committee on the Judiciary, *Defense of Marriage Act*, report to accompany H.R. 3396, 104th Cong., 2nd sess., July 9, 1996, H.Rept. 104-664 (Washington: GPO, 1996), p. 1.

[16] Ibid., p. 12.

[17] Ibid., p. 18.

[18] See, for example, Family Research Council, "Washington Update," February 23, 2012, at http://www.frc.org/washingtonupdate/at-opm-the-new-policy-is-berry-disturbing; and Cheryl Wetzstein, "Bill offers benefits to gay (continued...)

President Obama has issued two memoranda that address the eligibility of same-sex domestic partners for federal employee benefits. The first memorandum directed agencies to determine which benefits could be offered within the parameters of existing law. The second memorandum required agencies to extend specific benefits to the domestic partners of federal employees.

The First Memorandum

On June 17, 2009, President Obama released a memorandum directing all executive departments and agencies to review and evaluate their existing employee benefits to determine "which may legally be extended to same-sex partners."[19]

In his public statement accompanying the memorandum's release, he said that his Administration "was not authorized by existing Federal law to provide same-sex couples with the full range of benefits enjoyed by heterosexual married couples." The President said many private companies already offer such benefits to same-sex domestic partners, which "helps them compete for and retain the brightest and most talented employees. The Federal Government is at a disadvantage on that score right now, and change is long overdue."[20]

The memorandum required each executive department and agency to provide to the Director of OPM a report that included "a review of the benefits provided by their respective departments and agencies" in order "to determine what authority they have to extend such benefits to same-sex domestic partners of Federal employees." Agencies were given 90 days to complete their reviews. In addition, the memorandum instructed OPM to issue guidance regarding compliance with anti-discrimination policies in the hiring of federal employees (5 U.S.C. §2302(b)(10)). The memorandum was explicit in stating that all extensions of benefits and protections be "consistent with Federal law." No extension of benefits, therefore, could violate DOMA or any other law prohibiting the extension of benefits to same-sex domestic partners. The agency reports were due on September 15, 2009. OPM reviewed these reports and worked with the Department of Justice (DOJ) to recommend the extension of several federal benefits to the partners of federal employees in same-sex relationships.

The Second Memorandum

On June 2, 2010, President Obama released a memorandum that detailed the benefits OPM and DOJ recommended for extension to same-sex partners.[21] The memorandum stated that children of

---

(...continued)

partners," *The Washington Times*, May 14, 2012, at http://www.washingtontimes.com/news/2012/may/14/bill-offers-benefits-to-gay-partners/.

[19] President Barack Obama, *Memorandum for the Heads of Executive Departments and Agencies*, The White House: Office of the Press Secretary, Subject: Federal Benefits and Non-Discrimination, June 17, 2009, at http://www.whitehouse.gov/assets/documents/2009fedbenefits_mem_rel.pdf. See also, The White House: Office of the Press Secretary, "Statement by the President on the Presidential Memorandum on Federal Benefits and Non-Discrimination, and Support of the Lieberman-Baldwin Benefits Legislation," press release, June 17, 2009, at http://www.whitehouse.gov/the_press_office/Statement-by-the-President-on-the-Presidential-Memorandum-on-Federal-Benefits-and-Non-Discrimination-and-Support-of-the-Lieberman-Baldwin-Benefits-Legislation/.

[20] Ibid.

[21] President Barack Obama, *Memorandum for the Heads of Executive Department and Agencies*, the White House, Office of the Press Secretary, Extension of Benefits to Same-sex Domestic Partners of Federal Employees, (continued...)

---

same-sex partners fall "within the definition of 'child' for purposes of [f]ederal child-care subsidies, and, where appropriate, for child-care services."[22] Additionally, the memorandum required extension of the following benefits:

- A same-sex partner will be deemed to have an insurable interest in a federal employee with respect to survivor annuities under the Civil Service Retirement System and Federal Employee Retirement System (5 U.S.C. §§8339 and 8420).[23] The employee will no longer have to file an affidavit with OPM certifying that his or her domestic partner is financially dependent on the employee.

- A federal employee in a same-sex partnership is now eligible for 24 hours of unpaid leave when the child of a same-sex partner is dismissed early from school, a routine medical purpose, or the same-sex partner or his or her child needs medical care.

- The same-sex partner of a federal employee is now eligible to collect travel and relocation payments incurred as a result of a partner's new job or reassignment. The benefit is also extended to a same-sex partner's children.

- A same-sex partner and his or her children are now eligible to join a credit union, use a fitness facility, or participate in planning and counseling services that are currently extended to an opposite-sex spouse and family members.

The memorandum also required OPM to report annually to the President "on the progress of the agencies in implementing this memorandum until such time as all recommendations have been appropriately implemented."[24] Pursuant to the memorandum, the benefit extensions were effective immediately. Media reports noted "lukewarm" reaction from gay rights groups to the extension of "marginal" benefits.[25]

Survey of Particular Benefits

Both federal employees and federal annuitants have access to certain benefits. Some of these benefits can be transferred to spouses or other designated persons. In some cases, a federal employee's spouse may be explicitly authorized to receive a federal benefit. In other cases, a federal employee may designate a particular person to receive a federal benefit.

This section reviews benefits that cannot be extended to same-sex partners, others that are available to same-sex partners, and still others that have been made available to same-sex partners by the Obama Administration. These benefits have been mentioned in both current and previous legislation and executive-branch memoranda. **Table 1** summarizes some of the benefits provided

---

(...continued)

Washington, D.C., June 2, 2010, at http://www.whitehouse.gov/the-press-office/presidential-memorandum-extension-benefits-same-sex-domestic-partners-federal-emplo.

[22] Ibid., p. 1.

[23] Federal retirement benefits will be discussed in greater detail below.

[24] Ibid., p. 3.

[25] Ben Smith, "Obama to extend some benefits to same-sex partners," *Politico*, June 16, 2009, at http://www.politico.com/blogs/bensmith/0609/Obama_to_extend_benefits_to_samesex_partners.html.

to federal employees and their spouses. It also provides information on whether these benefits are available to the same-sex partners of federal employees.

Table 1. Some Benefits Available to Federal Employees and Their Spouses (as Defined by DOMA) and the Availability of These Benefits to the Same-Sex Partners of Federal Employees

Federal Employee Benefit	Availability
Health, Dental, and Vision Benefits	A spouse of a federal employee may receive health, dental, and vision insurance benefits. A same-sex domestic partner is ineligible for these benefits.
Federal Employees Compensation Act (FECA)	A spouse of a federal employee is eligible for survivor benefits if the employee is killed while performing his or her job. A same-sex domestic partner is not eligible to receive compensation under FECA.
Family and Medical Leave Act (FMLA)	Eligible employees may use unpaid leave to care for an ailing spouse or for the ailing child of a spouse. An eligible employee may use unpaid leave to care for an ailing same-sex domestic partner. An eligible employee may use unpaid leave to care for the child of a same-sex domestic partner.
Other Types of Leave (such as sick leave, funeral leave)	OPM regulations define "family member" for various types of leave. A spouse and a same-sex domestic partner are both included in the definition of "family member" for leave purposes.
Federal Employees' Group Life Insurance (FEGLI)	If a designated beneficiary is not named, a spouse automatically receives the life insurance benefit upon the death of a federal employee enrolled in FEGLI. A same-sex domestic partner would not automatically be the beneficiary. A federal employee may designate anyone, including a same-sex domestic partner, as the beneficiary of a life insurance benefit.
Civil Service Retirement System (CSRS) and Federal Employee Retirement System (FERS) Pensions and Survivors Benefits	A spouse may be entitled to receive a survivor's benefit under CSRS and FERS if the worker dies while employed in federal service or if the worker dies after retirement. The default benefit for a married federal worker who retires is a joint-and-survivor annuity. A same-sex domestic partner is ineligible to receive a survivor benefit and a federal worker with a same-sex domestic partner is not eligible to receive a joint-and-survivor annuity.
Insurable Interest Annuity	A federal employee may designate anyone who is financially dependent on the employee as the beneficiary of an Insurable Interest Annuity. A same-sex domestic partner may be designated as the beneficiary of an Insurable Interest Annuity.
Thrift Savings Plan (TSP)	A TSP participant may designate anyone, including a same-sex domestic partner, as the beneficiary of a TSP account. Upon death of the TSP participant, the TSP account is distributed based on order of precedence, if no beneficiary has been designated. In the order of precedence, "spouse" is listed first. "Same-sex domestic partner" is not listed in the order of precedence and would not be eligible to receive the proceeds of a TSP account if no beneficiary has been named.
Federal Long-Term Care Insurance Program (FLTCIP)	Qualified relatives of federal employees are eligible to enroll in the FLTCIP. Same-sex domestic partners are included in the definition of qualified relatives.

Source: 5 U.S.C. §8909; 5 C.F.R. §890; P.L. 108-496; 5 U.S.C. Chapter 89A and 5 U.S.C. Chapter 89B; 5 U.S.C. Chapter 81; P.L. 103-3; 5 U.S.C. Chapter 63; 5 U.S.C. Chapter 87; P.L. 106-265; 5 U.S.C. §9001.

Benefits Expressly Provided to Spouses

Health Benefits

The Federal Employees Health Benefits Program (FEHBP; 5 U.S.C. §8909; 5 C.F.R. §890) offers health benefits to qualifying federal employees and encompasses nearly 300 different health care plans. As with health care plans in the private sector, FEHBP provides benefits to enrollees for costs associated with a health checkup, an injury, or an illness. Health care costs are shared between the federal government and the enrollee. According to a 2010 study, the federal government pays, on average, 72% of a health plan's premium and 28% of the premium's cost is paid by the employee.[26]

Pursuant to the *Code of Federal Regulations*, certain family members of a federal employee are eligible to enroll in FEHBP.[27] Among those eligible are an employee's spouse and children under age 22.[28]

Neither same-sex domestic partners of federal employees nor the partners' children are eligible to enroll in FEHBP.[29] OPM's website states the following:

> Same sex partners are not eligible family members. The law defines family members as a spouse and an unmarried dependent child under age 22. P.L. 104-199, Defense of Marriage Act, states, "the word 'marriage' means only a legal union between one man and one woman as husband and wife, and the word 'spouse' refers only to a person of the opposite sex who is a husband or a wife."[30]

Dental and Vision Benefits

Federal employees may choose to enroll in the Federal Dental and Vision Program (FEDVIP; P.L. 108-496; 5 U.S.C. Chapter 89A and 5 U.S.C. Chapter 89B), which provides vision and dental benefits in addition to the limited coverage provided by FEHBP. Unlike FEHBP, however,

---

[26] U.S. Government Accountability Office, *U.S. Postal Service: Strategies and Options to Facilitate Progress toward Financial Viability*, GAO-10-455, p. 28, April 2010, at http://www.gao.gov/new.items/d10455.pdf. This average does not include the health benefit costs for the U.S. Postal Service (USPS). The health care benefits cost for USPS's nearly 646,000 employees is borne by USPS and its employees. Historically, USPS has paid a larger share of employees' health insurance premiums compared to other federal agencies. Until January 2012, USPS paid all health benefits costs for officers and executives of the service. In January, USPS's share of officer and executive health benefits premiums dropped from 100% to 91%. Over the next two years, the percentage of the premium covered by USPS will continue to drop until that percentage is equal to what the federal government provides to its other employees (an average of 72%).

[27] 5 C.F.R. §890.302.

[28] Ibid. A federal employee's child includes a "legitimate child," "an adopted child," or a "stepchild, foster child, or recognized natural child who lives with the enrollee in a regular parent-child relationship." As of January 1, 2011, an eligible dependent child may be up to 26 years old, pursuant to P.L. 111-148, the Patient Protection and Affordable Care Act. For more information see U.S. Office of Personnel Management, "Health: Reform," at http://www.opm.gov/insure/health/reform/index.asp.

[29] If a federal employee legally adopted the child of his or her same-sex partner, the child would be eligible to receive federal benefits. 5 C.F.R. §890.302.

[30] U.S. Office of Personnel Management, "Federal Employees Health Benefits Program Handbook," at http://www.opm.gov/insure/health/reference/handbook/fehb28.asp.

---

the enrollee pays all benefit premium costs—the federal government does not contribute to the benefit's premiums.

Like federal health benefits, federal employees may extend FEDVIP benefits to family members. Eligibility rules are identical to FEHBP's regulations.[31]

Both the Enhanced Dental Benefits program (5 U.S.C. §8951) and the Enhanced Vision Benefits program (5 U.S.C. §8981) are not extended to the same-sex partners of federal employees who are eligible for the benefit. OPM states on its website that "[t]he rules for family members' eligibility are the same as they are for the" FEHBP for both the dental and the vision programs.[32]

Federal Employment Compensation Act Benefits

A federal employee is eligible for up to $100,000 in compensation if he or she is disabled while performing his or her job, pursuant to the Federal Employment Compensation Act (FECA; 5 U.S.C. Chapter §§8101-8193). If an employee is killed while performing his or her job, 5 U.S.C. §8102a requires that payment go to the deceased employee's spouse or children. The federal employee may also designate his or her parents or siblings as the compensation recipient.[33] The same-sex partner of a federal employee is not listed in statute among the eligible recipients of such compensation.

Federal Benefits Provided to Spouses and Others

As noted earlier, for certain benefits, the term *spouse* is either not found in the benefit's authorizing language or the authorizing language widens the scope of eligibility. This section describes federal benefits that are either explicitly extended to same-sex partners of federal employees or those that allow federal employees to designate same-sex partners as beneficiaries.

Family and Medical Leave Act

Pursuant to the Family and Medical Leave Act (FMLA; P.L. 103-3; 5 U.S.C. Chapter 63), certain[34] federal employees are entitled to use up to 12 weeks of unpaid leave during any 12-month period for any of the following reasons:

- the birth of a child of the employee and follow-up care related to that birth;

- the adoption of a child by the employee or placement of a foster child with the employee;

- the care of an employee's ailing spouse, child, or parent;

---

[31] U.S. Office of Personnel Management, "Federal Employees Dental and Vision Insurance Program (FEDVIP)," at http://www.opm.gov/insure/archive/dentalvision/.

[32] U.S. Office of Personnel Management, "Dental: Introduction," at http://www.opm.gov/insure/dental/index.asp; and U.S. Office of Personnel Management, "Vision: Introduction," at http://www.opm.gov/insure/vision/index.asp.

[33] 5 U.S.C. §8102a(d)(1).

[34] Pursuant to FMLA, federal employees must have completed at least one year of federal civilian service to qualify for leave. Additionally, temporary and intermittent employees are not excluded from FMLA coverage (5 U.S.C. §6382).

- an illness or condition of the employee that renders him or her unable to work; or

- the spouse, child, or parent of the employee is on covered active duty or has been notified of an impending call or order to covered active duty in the Armed Forces.[35]

The 12 weeks of unpaid leave may be used intermittently throughout the year, when the employee meets statutory and regulatory requirements of FMLA.[36]

FMLA regulations (5 C.F.R. §630.1201) define *spouse* explicitly as "an individual who is a husband or wife pursuant to a marriage that is a legal union between one man and one woman, including common law marriage between one man and one woman in States where it is recognized." A federal employee, therefore, may not use leave acquired pursuant to FMLA to care for an ailing same-sex domestic partner.

A June 22, 2010, Department of Labor (DOL) Administrator Interpretation of FMLA interpreted the act's definition of "son or daughter" to permit an employee in a same-sex partnership to use FMLA-approved leave to care for the child of his or her same-sex partner.[37] Prior to the Administrator Interpretation, a federal employee was not permitted to use leave acquired pursuant to FMLA to care for the ailing child of a same-sex domestic partner, unless the employee had legally adopted the child. The DOL interpretation applies to all employees in both the public and private sectors.

Other Types of Leave

On June 14, 2010, OPM released a final rule clarifying the definitions of *family member* and *immediate relative* as they are used in determining eligibility for certain kinds of leave— including sick leave, funeral leave, voluntary leave transfer, voluntary leave bank, and emergency leave transfer.[38] The regulation formerly had defined "family member" as any one of the following:

- spouse, and parents thereof;

- children, including adopted children and spouses thereof;

- parents;

---

[35] Pursuant to FMLA, a federal employee whose "spouse, son, daughter, parent, or next of kin" is a covered servicemember "shall be entitled to a total of 26 administrative workweeks of leave during a 12-month period to care for the servicemember" (5 U.S.C. §6382).

[36] Pursuant to FMLA, federal employees are required to give employers at least 30 days' notice prior to taking leave when the need for leave is foreseeable (5 U.S.C. §6382(e)).

[37] Deputy Administrator Nancy J. Leppink, *Administrator's Interpretation No. 2010-3*, U.S. Department of Labor, June 22, 2010, at http://www.dol.gov/whd/opinion/adminIntrprtn/FMLA/2010/FMLAAI2010_3.pdf. The interpretation permits any person serving "in loco parentis" to use FMLA-approved leave to care for a child. The interpretation defines "in loco parentis" as someone "who has put himself in the situation of a lawful parent by assuming the obligations incident to the parental relation without going through the formalities necessary to legal adoption." The new definition, therefore, is to include any adult-child relationship in which an adult is not the legal or biological parent of a child but he or she "has day-to-day responsibility for caring for a child."

[38] U.S. Office of Personnel Management, "Absence and Leave; Definition of Family Member, Immediate Relative, and Related Terms," 75 *Federal Register* 33491-33497, June 14, 2010.

- brothers and sisters; and

- any individual related by blood or affinity whose close association with the employee is the equivalent of a family relationship.[39]

Pursuant to the new regulation, the definition of family member now also includes

- grandparents and grandchildren, and spouses thereof; and

- a domestic partner and parents thereof, including the domestic partner of any of the relatives listed above.[40]

The new regulation also modified existing or added new definitions to criteria that determine if same-sex partners would be eligible for certain leave benefits. For example, the terms *committed relationship*,[41] *domestic partner*,[42] *parent*,[43] and *son or daughter*[44] were added into the *Code of Federal Regulations*. The modified regulation applies to leave benefits for both same-sex and opposite-sex partnerships, and includes but is not limited to partnerships recognized by a state, territory, or district government. The regulation became effective June 14, 2010. The regulation does not appear to affect FMLA.

Life Insurance

In some cases, a federal employee may not choose to enroll a spouse or same-sex partner in a federal benefit program. Instead, the employee may designate any individual as the recipient of a federal benefit. Pursuant to 5 U.S.C. Chapter 87, most federal employees, including part-time employees, are automatically enrolled in the Federal Employees' Group Life Insurance (FEGLI) program, which is administered by Metropolitan Life Insurance Company.[45] Federal employees pay two-thirds of their life-insurance premium, and the federal government pays the remaining third.[46] A federal employee may designate anyone, including a same-sex partner, as their life insurance beneficiary by filing an SF 2823 form.[47] A federal employee's spouse would

---

[39] 5 C.F.R. §630.201. The definition of "immediate relative" was identically modified in 5 C.F.R. §630.803. The definitions of "committed relationship," "domestic partner," "family member," "parent," and "son or daughter" were modified in or added to 5 C.F.R. §630.902.

[40] Ibid., p. 33495.

[41] Ibid., p. 33496. The regulation defined the term as follows:

> [a relationship] in which the employee, and the domestic partner of the employee, are each other's sole domestic partner (and are not married to or domestic partners with anyone else); and share responsibility for a significant measure of each other's common welfare and financial obligations. This includes, but is not limited to, any relationship between two individuals of the same or opposite sex that is granted legal recognition by a State or by the District of Columbia as a marriage or analogous relationship (including, but not limited to, a civil union).

[42] Ibid. The regulation defined the term as follows: "[A]n adult in a committed relationship with another adult, including both same-sex and opposite-sex relationships."

[43] Ibid. The regulation modified the term by adding a "parent … of an employee's spouse or domestic partner."

[44] Ibid. The regulation modified the term by adding a "son or daughter … of an employee's spouse or domestic partner."

[45] A qualifying federal employee may be exempted from the life insurance program if he or she provides required written notice of the desired exemption (5 U.S.C. §8702). Qualifying federal employees may choose to enroll in additional life insurance coverage.

[46] USPS pays 100% of the life insurance premium.

[47] For more information about the SF 2823, see U.S. Office of Personnel Management, "Life: Designation of (continued...)

---

automatically receive the federal benefit if he or she did not specifically designate a different beneficiary, pursuant to federal law (5 U.S.C. §8705(a)).

In 5 U.S.C. §8701, the section of *U.S. Code* that defines the terms used on statutes that govern federal life insurance, *family member* includes the phrase *spouse of the individual* when listing eligible beneficiaries. Title 5 U.S.C. §8705, the section of code that delineates the order of preference in which life insurance benefits would be distributed in the event of a federal employee's death, says life insurance benefits would first be distributed to any person or entity that was selected by the employee using the SF 2823 form. If no form was completed, the benefit would then go to "the widow or widower of the employee."[48] It would appear, therefore, that DOMA would preclude same-sex domestic partners from qualifying as a widow or widower.

Federal Employee Pensions and Survivor Benefits

Federal employees with permanent appointments are eligible for retirement and disability benefits under either CSRS or FERS.[49] Employees hired before January 1, 1984, are covered by CSRS unless they chose to switch to FERS during open seasons held in 1987 and 1998. Most federal employees initially hired into permanent federal employment on or after January 1, 1984, are covered by FERS. CSRS and FERS provide (1) a defined benefit pension plan, which pays a monthly dollar amount for the lifetime of the retiree; and (2) access to the Thrift Savings Plan (TSP), which is a defined contribution retirement savings plan in which employee and (for employees covered by FERS) agency contributions accrue tax-deferred investment earnings in a retirement savings account.

Benefits Under CSRS/FERS Defined Benefit Pension Plan

Workers covered by the CSRS or FERS defined benefit pension plan receive a monthly retirement annuity for the lifetime of the retiree if the retiree meets all eligibility requirements. The payment in retirement is determined by a formula that uses the worker's number of years in federal service, an accrual percentage, and salary base.[50] The accrual rate is higher for employees under CSRS than under FERS. Workers covered by CSRS do not participate in Social Security, do not receive Social Security benefits, and do not pay Social Security taxes. Workers covered by FERS fully participate in Social Security.[51]

Under CSRS and FERS, an eligible spouse is entitled to receive monthly retirement benefits if (1) the covered worker dies while employed in federal service; or (2) the covered worker dies after

---

(...continued)

Beneficiary," at http://www.opm.gov/insure/life/fegli/sf2823.asp.

[48] 5 U.S.C. §8705(a).

[49] For more information, see CRS Report 98-810, *Federal Employees' Retirement System: Benefits and Financing*, by Katelin P. Isaacs.

[50] For example, CSRS pensions equal 1.5% of high-three average pay for each of the first five years of service, 1.75% for the 6th through 10th years; and 2.0% of high-three average pay for each year of service after the 10th year. FERS pensions equal 1% of high-three year average pay for each year of service or 1.1% per year of service if the employee retires at age 62 or older and has 20 or more years of federal service. Current Members of Congress and congressional staff, federal law enforcement officers, firefighters, and air traffic controllers accrue benefits at higher rates.

[51] Some Members of Congress can opt out of the federal pension plan and choose to be covered by Social Security alone. See CRS Report RL30631, *Retirement Benefits for Members of Congress*, by Katelin P. Isaacs.

---

retirement. When a federal employee dies, the surviving spouse of the deceased federal employee may be entitled to a survivor's benefit.[52] When a married federal worker retires, the married couple receives a monthly retirement benefit for the longer of the lifetime of the worker or the spouse. The monthly benefit in retirement is reduced to account for the expected longer time period in which the benefit will be paid. The spousal benefit is the default option for married federal employees, unless both the federal worker and spouse provide written consent to waive the benefit.

Title 5 of the *U.S. Code*, which governs benefits under CSRS and FERS, defines the term *spouse* without reference to the individual's gender. Title 5 does not define the word *marriage*; however, the *Code of Federal Regulations* defines *marriage* for purposes of determining eligibility for federal retirement benefits under Title 5 as "a marriage recognized in law or equity under the whole law of the jurisdiction with the most significant interest in the marital status of the employee, member, or retiree unless the law of that jurisdiction is contrary to the public policy of the United States."[53] Since DOMA defines a *spouse* as "a person of the opposite sex who is a husband or a wife," same-sex partners are ineligible to receive spousal benefits entitled to opposite-sex partners.

If a federal employee dies, and no survivor annuity is payable to a spouse, former spouse, or a child, then the employee's contributions to CSRS and FERS may be returned as a lump-sum benefit. Under both FERS and CSRS, an employee may designate anyone, including a same-sex partner, as his or her beneficiary for a lump-sum refund of retirement contributions to the retirement system. If anyone qualifies to receive survivor annuity benefits by law (such as a spouse or dependent child), however, retirement contributions cannot be refunded. If no survivor benefit is payable and the employee has not designated a beneficiary, then the return of contributions will be distributed based on the order of precedence. The order of precedence awards the benefits in the following order: widow or widower; child or children equally, and to the descendants of deceased children; parents equally or surviving parent; appointed executor or administrator of estate; or next of kin who is entitled to your estate under the laws of the state in which the employee resided at the time of death.

Insurable Interest Annuity

Although a federal employee cannot name a domestic partner as his or her surviving beneficiary under either FERS or CSRS, an employee who is applying for a non-disability retirement can elect an Insurable Interest Annuity (IIA), which is a survivor annuity to an individual who is financially dependent on the employee. Only one person may be named as the beneficiary of the IIA, and the election must be made at the time of retirement. The employee must establish, through one or more affidavits from other people, the reasons why the beneficiary might reasonably expect to suffer loss of financial support as a result of the employee's death. The cost of an IIA can range from a 10% reduction in the employee's retirement annuity if the beneficiary

---

[52] Under CSRS, survivor benefits are paid to the surviving spouse if the employee completed at least 18 months of creditable service and was covered under CSRS at the time of death. Under FERS, survivor benefits are paid to the surviving spouse if the employee completed at least 18 months of creditable civilian service under FERS. Under both CSRS and FERS, the surviving spouse must be married to the employee for at least nine months. If the death occurred before nine months of marriage, a survivor annuity may still be payable if the employee's death was accidental, or if there was a child born of the marriage. For details on the amount of the survivor's benefit, see http://www.opm.gov/retire/post/survivor/deceased_employee.asp.

[53] See 5 C.F.R. §831.603 and 5 C.F.R. §843.10.

is 10 years younger than the employee to a 40% reduction if the beneficiary is 30 or more years younger.

TSP Defined Contribution Pension Plan

Both CSRS- and FERS-covered workers may contribute up to $17,000 in 2012 ($22,500 for those age 50 and older) to the Thrift Savings Plan (TSP). Contributions to TSP are excluded from taxable income; taxes are paid when funds are withdrawn in retirement. Employees covered by FERS receive an agency matching contribution of up to 5% to their TSP account. Workers covered by CSRS do not receive agency matching contributions.

A federal employee can name anyone, including a domestic partner, as the beneficiary under the TSP.[54] The beneficiary will receive the amount in the TSP account following a participant's death. For spouses who are beneficiaries of a deceased TSP participant and the account is $200 or more, TSP establishes a beneficiary participant account. The beneficiary account is automatically invested in the Government Securities Investment (G) Fund until the spouse beneficiary elects different investment options. The spouse may keep the funds in the TSP beneficiary account or elect to withdraw or transfer the funds to an Individual Retirement Account (IRA) or other retirement plan, if the plan allows. Non-spouse beneficiaries cannot retain a TSP account. The funds in a deceased participant's account are either transferred directly to the non-spouse beneficiary or to an inherited IRA.[55]

Death Benefits If No Beneficiary Is Named

If an employee does not designate one or more beneficiaries under FERS, CSRS, or the TSP, the funds will be distributed based on the order of precedence. The order of precedence awards the benefits in the following order: widow or widower; child or children equally, and to the descendants of deceased children; parents equally or surviving parent; appointed executor or administrator of estate; or next of kin who is entitled to the estate under the laws of the state in which the employee resided at the time of death. Thus, the funds from the TSP or CSRS/FERS lump-sum benefit will bypass a same-sex partner unless the federal employee actively designates that person as the beneficiary.[56]

Federal Long Term Care

Federal employees may apply for the Federal Long Term Care Insurance Program (FLTCIP; P.L. 106-265; 5 U.S.C. §9001), which provides medical services for enrollees who suffer a chronic medical condition and are unable to care for themselves. Employees may voluntarily opt into FLTCIP, and the entire premium is covered by the enrollee. Pursuant to 5 U.S.C. §9001, qualifying federal employees; members of the uniformed services; federal annuitants; current spouses of federal employees, servicemembers, or annuitants; adult children of federal employees, servicemembers, or annuitants; and parents, parents-in-law, and stepparents of federal

---

[54] For more information, see the TSP publication "Information for Participants and Beneficiaries," at https://www.tsp.gov/PDF/formspubs/tspbk31.pdf.

[55] For more information on IRAs, see CRS Report RL34397, *Traditional and Roth Individual Retirement Accounts (IRAs): A Primer*, by John J. Topoleski.

[56] 5 U.S.C. §5570.

employees, servicemembers, or annuitants are eligible to enroll in FLTCIP. In addition, federal law states that OPM may prescribe regulations that permit an "individual having such other relationship" to a federal employee, servicemember, or annuitant to enroll in FLTCIP.[57]

On June 1, 2010, OPM published in the *Federal Register* a final rule that expanded the definition of *qualified relative* to include "the same-sex domestic partners of eligible Federal and U.S. Postal Service employees and annuitants."[58] As of July 1, 2010, same-sex partners of federal employees are eligible for FLTCIP benefits.

Several comments received by OPM during the regulatory review of the definition change of *qualified relative* requested that opposite-sex domestic partners—in addition to same-sex partners—be made eligible for the long term care benefit. In the final rule, however, OPM wrote that "opposite-sex domestic partners were not included because they may obtain eligibility to apply for Federal long term care insurance through marriage, an option not currently available to same-sex domestic partners."[59]

Legislation in the 112th Congress

In the 112th Congress, two bills have been introduced that, if enacted, would provide insurance, travel, and other benefits to the same-sex partners of federal employees. On November 18, 2011, Senator Joe Lieberman—on behalf of himself and Senator Susan Collins—introduced S. 1910, the Domestic Partnership Benefits and Obligations Act of 2011. That same day, Representative Tammy Baldwin introduced a companion bill, H.R. 3485, in the House. S. 1910 was referred to the Committee on Homeland Security and Governmental Affairs. On May 16, 2012, the committee reported S. 1910 favorably with an amendment in the nature of a substitute.[60] H.R. 3485 was referred to the Oversight and Government Reform Committee's Subcommittee on Workforce Protections, the House Education and the Workforce's Subcommittee on Workforce Protections, the House Judiciary's Subcommittee on Courts, Commercial and Administrative

---

[57] 5 U.S.C. §9001(5)(D).

[58] U.S. Office of Personnel Management, "Federal Long Term Care Insurance Program: Eligibility Changes," 75 *Federal Register* 30267-30268, June 1, 2010. According to the final rule, "domestic partner" is defined as follows:

> "domestic partner" is a person in a domestic partnership with an employee or annuitant of the same sex. The term "domestic partnership" is defined as a committed relationship between two adults, of the same sex, in which the partners—are each other's sole domestic partner and intend to remain so indefinitely; have a common residence, and intend to continue the arrangement indefinitely; are at least 18 years of age and mentally competent to consent to contract; share responsibility for a significant measure of each other's financial obligations; are not married to anyone else; are not a domestic partner of anyone else; are not related in a way that, if they were of opposite sex, would prohibit legal marriage in the state in which they reside; will certify they understand that willful falsification of the documentation described in paragraph (a) of this section may lead to disciplinary action and the recovery of the cost of benefits received related to such falsification and may constitute a criminal violation under 18 U.S.C. § 1001.

Prior to this regulation, qualified relatives included a spouse, parent, stepparent, parent-in-law, and adult child who was at least age 18.

[59] Ibid., p. 30267.

[60] The amendment added a provision that allowed the federal government to recoup certain health costs if those costs were paid for by an outside insurer or other liable entity. It also provided authority to pay for the costs of same-sex partner benefits, as well as included some technical amendments.

Law, and the Committee on House Administration. No further action has been taken on H.R. 3485.

Among the benefits the bills[61] sought to extend were the following:

- health insurance and enhanced dental and vision benefits (5 U.S.C. Chapters 89, 89A, 89B);

- retirement and disability benefits and plans (5 U.S.C. Chapters 83, 84; 31 U.S.C Chapter 7; 50 U.S.C. Chapter 38);

- family, medical, and emergency leave (2 U.S.C. §1312; 3 U.S.C. §412; 5 U.S.C. Chapter 63 – subchapters II, IV, and V; 29 U.S.C. §2601 et seq.);

- federal group life insurance (5 U.S.C. Chapter 87);

- long-term care insurance (5 U.S.C. Chapter 90);

- compensation for work injuries (5 U.S.C. Chapter 81);

- benefits for disability, death, or captivity (5 U.S.C. §§5569 and 5570; 22 U.S.C. §3973; 42 U.S.C. §3796 et seq.); and

- travel, transportation, and related payments and benefits (5 U.S.C. Chapter 57; 22 U.S.C. §4981 et seq.; 10 U.S.C. §1599b; 22 U.S.C. Chapter 52; 33 U.S.C. §3071).[62]

Pursuant to S. 1910, each qualifying federal employee seeking to enroll his or her same-sex domestic partner in a federal benefit program would have been required to file an affidavit of eligibility with OPM. In the affidavit, the employee would have had "attest" that he or she was in a "committed domestic-partnership," which included the following conditions:

- the partners "are in a committed domestic-partnership relationship with each other ... and intend to remain so indefinitely";

- the partners "have a common residence and intend to continue to do so";[63]

- the partners are at least 18 years old and are "mentally competent to consent to contract";

- the partners "share responsibility for a significant measure of each other's common welfare and financial obligations";

---

[61] This section of the report defaults to bill language in S. 1910, unless otherwise stated. In some instances, the language in S. 1910 was identical or similar to the language in H.R. 3485. In some instances, the bills had different language. This section of the report included examples of both similar and different language uses in the bills. The report makes clear when language from H.R. 3485 was provided.

[62] Not all of the sections of U.S. Code cited in this list are explicitly included in S. 1910 and H.R. 3485. For example, disability, death, or captivity benefits for Foreign Service officers and public safety officers (22 U.S.C. §3973 and 42 U.S.C. §3796, respectively).

[63] H.R. 3485 would have allowed the partners to live in separate locations "because of financial, employment-related, or other reasons identified in the affidavit." S. 1910, on the other hand, included language that permitted the partners to live in separate residences when they were "prevented from [living together] because of an assignment abroad or other employment-related factors, financial considerations, family responsibilities, or other similar reason" that would be identified in the affidavit.

- the partners are not "married to or in a domestic partnership with anyone except each other";

- the partners are not related by blood in a way that would prohibit legal marriage between individuals otherwise eligible to marry in the jurisdiction"; and

- the partners would be subject to the same ethical standards, financial disclosures, and conflict of interest requirements as those placed on the spouses of federal employees (5 U.S.C. Appendix; 5 U.S.C. §§3110, 7301, 7342(a)(1),7351, 7353; 2 U.S.C. §1602(4)(D); 18 U.S.C. §§205(e), 208(a); 31 U.S.C. §1353; 42 U.S.C. §290b(j)(2)).

Additionally, the applicant would have had to attest that he or she understood that "as a domestic partner, each individual not only gains certain benefits, but also assumes some obligations." The bills' language provided for "criminal and other penalties" if certain legal obligations were violated.[64]

Both S. 1910 and H.R. 3485 would have required a federal employee to file a statement of dissolution within 30 days of the death of his or her same-sex partner or the dissolution of the relationship.[65] Both bills would have provided benefits to the living partner of a deceased federal employee as if he or she were a widow or widower.[66] Additionally, a former partner would have been entitled to benefits identical to that of a former spouse.[67]

Natural children or adopted step children of a federal employee's same-sex partner would have been entitled to benefits identical to that of a natural or adopted child of a federal employee's spouse, pursuant to the bills.[68]

Similar bills to both S. 1910 and H.R. 3485 were introduced in the previous seven Congresses.[69]

No bill has been introduced in the 112th Congress that sought to explicitly rescind the benefits extended by the Obama Administration.

---

[64] S. 1910, Section 101. H.R. 3485's language was different than that in S. 1910. H.R. 3485 read as follows:

> The filing employee, former employee, or annuitant (as the case may be) understands that willful falsification of information set forth in the affidavit or failure to provide appropriate notification of the termination of the domestic partnership may lead to the recovery of amounts obtained as a result of such falsification or failure (as the case may be), criminal or other penalties, and (in appropriate cases) disciplinary action.

[65] Defining the term "dissolution" may prove difficult. In an opposite-sex marriage, the dissolution of the relationship is determined by law. As many same-sex partnerships are recognized in limited circumstances or not at all, the dissolution of such unions may vary based on jurisdiction. Moreover, the dissolution of partnerships entered into in other jurisdictions may prove problematic. Determining when a same-sex relationship is officially dissolved is beyond the scope of this report.

[66] Title II of S. 1910 includes language that would extend these benefits to employees covered by CSRS (Section 205), while Title III would extend the benefits for federal employees covered by FERS (Section 315).

[67] Ibid.

[68] See, for example, in S. 1910 Sec. 3182(2)(B), which discusses benefits under FERS.

[69] H.R. 2517 and S. 1102 in the 111th Congress; H.R. 4838 and S. 2521 in the 110th Congress; H.R. 3267 in and S. 3955 in the 109th Congress; H.R. 2426 and S. 1252 in the 108th Congress; H.R. 638 and S. 2874 in the 107th Congress; H.R. 2859 in the 106th Congress; H.R. 2761 and S. 1636 in the 105th Congress.

Some Potential Policy Considerations Regarding Same-Sex Benefits and Federal Employees

This section provides analysis of some potential policy considerations Congress may consider that are related to federal employees and the extension of health and other benefits to same-sex partners of federal employees. Congress may choose to examine or modify existing policies related to the extension of benefits to the partners of federal employees in same-sex relationships, or maintain existing policies. Currently benefits like health care, dental care and eye care are not available to the same-sex partner of a federal employee. Other benefits, like FMLA and life insurance, however, are.

The Obama Administration has pledged its support for extending federal benefits to the same-sex partners of federal employees. The Administration has extended some benefits to same-sex partners and has argued that its actions are within the parameters of existing laws. DOMA, which was enacted by Congress and signed into law by President William J. Clinton, requires agencies to define *spouse* as a person of the opposite-sex, for the purpose of distributing federal benefits. [70]

Attracting and Hiring the Most Effective Employees

Some may worry that not providing same-sex partner benefits makes the federal government a less attractive employment option to potential employees who have same-sex partners. They contend that to compete for the most effective and efficient workforce the federal government needs to offer benefits similar to those available in state and local governments and in the private sector. [71] The Obama Administration, for example, has argued that by not extending same-sex benefits, the federal government faces difficulties recruiting and retaining high-performing

---

[70] In December 2009, although a federal court ordered OPM to do so, OPM reportedly decided not to extend benefits to the same-sex partners of judicial branch federal employees who are married in California. The agency reportedly stated that extending such benefits would be a violation of existing federal law (DOMA). See Joe Davidson, "OPM Defies Order on Same-sex Benefits," *Washington Post*, December 22, 2009, at http://www.washingtonpost.com/wp-dyn/content/article/2009/12/21/AR2009122103240.html.

[71] As noted earlier in this report, in congressional testimony Ms. Badgett said more than 250 cities, counties, and other local governments provide same-sex domestic partners with benefits. In the private sector, almost two-thirds of the Fortune 1000, and 83% of Fortune 100 companies provide such benefits. U.S. Congress, House Committee on Oversight and Government Reform, Subcommittee on Federal Workforce, Post Office, and the District of Columbia, *Domestic Partnership Benefits and Obligations Act of 2009*, hearing on H.R. 2517, 111th Cong., 1st sess., July 8, 2009 (Washington: GPO, 2009), at http://republicans.oversight.house.gov/images/stories/Hearings/pdfs/20090708Badgett.pdf. Academic studies have shown that employees are attracted to jobs that offer optimal compensation packages, which includes benefits. See, for example, Robert R. Sinclair, Michael C. Leo, and Chris Wright, "Benefit System Effects on Employees' Benefit Knowledge, Use, and Organizational Commitment," *Journal of Business and Psychology*, vol. 20, no. 1 (Fall 2005), pp. 3-29. In December 2007, the Center for State and Local Governance commissioned a public opinion poll asking 1,200 Americans what made a job attractive. The results showed that health care benefits rated much higher than salary. See Princeton Survey Research Associates International, *Data Report: Security: What Americans want from a job*, December 2007, http://slge.org/wp-content/uploads/2012/01/Security_What_Americans_Want_from_a_Job1.pdf. Other academic articles operate from the assumption that workers are attracted to benefits, see, for example Thomas T. Robertson and Steven A. Harrold, "Tailoring benefits to attract effective managers," *Journal (American Water Works Association)*, December 1983, pp. 592-595. Still other academic studies note explicitly that employers assume benefits will attract the employees, see Margaret A. Lucero and Robert E. Allen, "Employee Benefits: A Growing Source of Psychological Contract Violations," *Human Resource Management*, vol. 33, no. 3 (Fall 1994), p. 428.

---

employees who are in or who may enter into same-sex relationships. Such employees may instead choose to work for state, local, or tribal governments or private companies that provide benefits to same-sex domestic partners. When Congress enacted DOMA, report language that accompanied the legislation did not address whether denying such benefits could impede the federal government's ability to hire the most effective workers. At the time of DOMA's enactment, few employers offered same-sex benefits to their employees. There is no federal data that has tracked, over time, the availability of same-sex partner benefits to either public or private-sector employees.[72] Such data could aid in the determination of whether private-sector employers or other levels of government have been offering benefits that the federal government has not.[73]

Domestic Partner Benefits in the Public and Private Sector

Some private-sector and public-sector employers offer benefits to the domestic partners[74] of their employees. The types and scope of the benefits offered, however, vary: some employers provide only health care benefits to domestic partners while other employers provide additional benefits—such as survivorship benefits under the employer's pension plan.[75] A Congressional Research Service search of academic, legal, and other research databases, found that there appear to be few studies that track, over time, how many employers provide same-sex partner benefits to their employees and the scope of those benefits. Some studies, however, provide benefits data for a single date or over a short time span. This section provides data from these surveys.

When DOMA was enacted, few employers in the private and public sector offered domestic partner benefits of any sort. For example, a study by Hewitt Associates LLC, a global management consulting company, found in 1997 that 10% of 570 large U.S. employers offered domestic partner benefits. In 2000, the percentage of companies surveyed by Hewitt that offered domestic partner benefits increased to 22%.[76] According to the National Survey of Employer-Sponsored Health Plans conducted by Mercer, a global consulting company, 46% of corporations

---

[72] In July 2011, the Bureau of Labor Statistics, for the first time in its history, "produced data on employer-provided benefits available to unmarried domestic partners." See U.S. Department of Labor, Bureau of Labor Statistics, "Employee Benefits in the United States - March 2011," press release, July 26, 2011, at http://www.bls.gov/news.release/pdf/ebs2.pdf. Data for this survey are from BLS's National Compensation Survey and contain "data on civilian, private industry, and state and local government workers in the United States." For additional technical information on the data, see Bureau of Labor Statistics, "Economic News Release: Employee Benefits Technical Note," at http://www.bls.gov/news.release/ebs2.tn.htm.

[73] OPM Director John Berry stated in his July 8, 2009, testimony before the House Committee on Oversight and Government Reform's Subcommittee on Federal Workforce, Post Office, and the District of Columbia that extending federal benefits to same-sex partners of federal employees (pursuant to H.R. 2517 in the 111th Congress) would provide the federal government with a "a recruitment and retention tool." See U.S. Congress, House Committee on Oversight and Government Reform, Subcommittee on Federal Workforce, Post Office, and the District of Columbia, *The Domestic Partnership Benefits and Obligations Act of 2009*, H.R. 2517, 111th Cong., 1st sess., July 8, 2009, at http://www.opm.gov/News_Events/congress/testimony/111thCongress/07_08_2009.asp.

[74] Most studies used the term "domestic partner" and not "same-sex partner." The terms are not interchangeable, as "domestic partner" usually includes opposite-sex unmarried partners. CRS, however, used studies on "domestic partner" benefits as a proxy for provision of "same-sex partner" benefits because "same-sex partners" are usually included in the category of "domestic partner" benefits.

[75] For more information on the legal considerations of same-sex partnerships and employee benefits in the private sector—including legal challenges to DOMA, see CRS Report R41998, *Same-Sex Marriage and Employee Benefit Plans: Legal Considerations*, by Jennifer Staman.

[76] *Benefit Programs for Domestic Partners & Same-Sex Spouses*, Hewitt Associates. Lincolnshire, Ill.: 1997 and 2000.

---

with 500 or more employees included same-sex domestic partners as eligible dependents in 2011, which was an increase from 39% in 2010.[77] In testimony before the House Committee on Oversight and Government Reform, Dr. M.V. Lee Badgett, the research director of the Williams Institute,[78] said that "[i]n the private sector, almost two-thirds of the Fortune 1000, and 83% of Fortune 100 companies" provide benefits to the same-sex partners of their employees and that 20 states, the District of Columbia, and "[m]ore than 250 cities, counties, and other local government entities cover domestic partners of other public employees."[79]

Many employers do not provide domestic-partner benefits. The nation's two largest private-sector employers—Walmart and Exxon Mobil—do not provide benefits to same-sex partners in the United States.[80] Other employers that provide benefits to same-sex partners—including I.B.M., Corning, and Raytheon—reportedly require same-sex couples to marry, if they live in a state where same-sex marriage is legal, to become eligible for health and other benefits.[81]

The Bureau of Labor Statistics Data

In 2011, the Bureau of Labor Statistics (BLS), for the first time in its history, released data on benefits provided to the domestic partners of employees.[82] In March 2012, BLS updated its survey data.[83] The BLS survey asked workers whether (1) they had access to a defined benefit pension plan at their place of employment and whether they had access to survivor benefits for an unmarried domestic partner and (2) they had access to health benefits at their place of

---

[77] See Mercer, "Employers Accelerate Efforts to Bring Health Benefit Costs Under Control," press release, November 16, 2011, at http://www.mercer.com/press-releases/national-survey-employer-sponsored-health-plans.

[78] The Williams Institute is a think tank at the University of California-Los Angeles that "advances sexual orientation and gender identity law and public policy through rigorous, independent research and scholarship." See the Williams Institute, "Mission," at http://williamsinstitute.law.ucla.edu/mission/.

[79] These states are Alaska, Arizona, California, Colorado, Connecticut, Illinois, Iowa, Maine, Maryland, Montana, Nevada, New Jersey, New Mexico, New York, Oregon, Pennsylvania, Rhode Island, Vermont, Washington, and Wisconsin. U.S. Congress, House Committee on Oversight and Government Reform, Subcommittee on Federal Workforce, Post Office, and the District of Columbia, *Domestic Partnership Benefits and Obligations Act of 2009*, hearing on H.R. 2517, 111th Cong., 1st sess., July 8, 2009 (Washington: GPO, 2009), at http://republicans.oversight.house.gov/images/stories/Hearings/pdfs/20090708Badgett.pdf.

[80] See, for example, Jenna Zwang, "Which Side do Companies Take in the Gay-Rights Culture War?" *National Journal*, September 27, 2011 at http://www.nationaljournal.com/pictures-video/which-side-do-companies-take-in-gay-rights-culture-war-pictures-20110927. On May 30, 2012, ExxonMobil shareholders rejected a resolution that would have required the company to amend its equal employment opportunity policy to prohibit discrimination based on sexual orientation and gender identity. The company indicated that it provides spousal benefits based on the definition of spouse in the country in which an employee resides. See Jon Street, "ExxonMobil Shareholders Vote No on Same-Sex Couple Benefits in USA," at http://cnsnews.com/news/article/exxonmobil-shareholders-vote-no-same-sex-couple-benefits-usa.

[81] Tara Siegel Bernard, "As Same-Sex Marriage Becomes Legal, Some Choices May be Lost," *New York Times*, July 8, 2011, at http://www.nytimes.com/2011/07/09/business/some-companies-want-gays-to-wed-to-get-health-benefits.html?_r=1.

[82] Bureau of Labor Statistics, "Employee Benefits in the United States, March 2011, Unmarried Domestic Partners Benefit Fact Sheet," July 26, 2011, at http://www.bls.gov/ncs/ebs/sp/ebs_domestic.pdf. Domestic partners include an unmarried couple of the opposite sex. The survey included 123 million workers from 12,545 establishments in the private sector and state and local governments. The survey does not include federal employees.

[83] Bureau of Labor Statistics, "Employee Benefits in the United States, March 2012, Unmarried Domestic Partners Benefit Fact Sheet, March 2012," at http://www.bls.gov/ncs/ebs_domestic2012.pdf. Domestic partners include an unmarried couple of the opposite sex. The survey included 123 million workers from 12,545 establishments in the private sector and state and local governments. The survey does not include federal employees.

---

employment and whether there was access for unmarried domestic partners. According to the surveys, workers in the public-sector (which would include state, local, and tribal—but not federal government) were more likely to be offered domestic partner benefits than workers in the private sector.[84]

BLS reported the following:

- Among private-sector workers with access to a defined benefit pension plan, 35% had access to survivorship benefits for a domestic partner in 2011 and 42% in 2012.

- Among private sector, civilian workers with access to health care benefits, 29% had access to health benefits for unmarried domestic partners in 2011. In 2012, the survey data was more granular. According to the data, 30% of private industry employees had access to health care benefits for a same-sex partner (as opposed to an opposite-sex domestic partner).

- Among workers who worked for state and local governments, 54% had access to health benefits for unmarried domestic partners.[85] In 2012, the survey data was more granular. According to the data, 33% of state and local government employees had access to benefits for a same-sex partner (as opposed to an opposite-sex domestic partner).[86]

Generally, the 2012 data demonstrated that health care benefits were "more prevalent for same-sex partners than for opposite-sex partners."[87]

Cost Estimates of Providing Domestic Partner Benefits to Federal Employees

In November 2012, CBO released its score of S. 1910, which, as described above, sought to extend certain benefits and responsibilities to the same-sex partners of federal employees and annuitants.[88] The score projected that the extension of benefits from FY2013 through FY2022 would cost the federal government $144 million in discretionary dollars over those 10 years.[89]

---

[84] Ibid.

[85] The data represent the percentage of workers with access to the benefit and not the percentage of employers who provide it. Because some states with large populations offer their employees domestic partner benefits, a greater percentage of state and local government workers have access to domestic partner benefits—even though a greater percentage of states do not provide these benefits.

[86] Bureau of Labor Statistics, "Employee Benefits in the United States, March 2011, Unmarried Domestic Partners Benefit Fact Sheet," July 26, 2011; and Bureau of Labor Statistics, "Employee Benefits in the United States, March 2012, Unmarried Domestic Partners Benefit Fact Sheet, March 2012."

[87] Bureau of Labor Statistics, "Employee Benefits in the United States, March 2012, Unmarried Domestic Partners Benefit Fact Sheet, March 2012."

[88] Congressional Budget Office, *S. 1910: Domestic Partners Benefits and Obligations Act of 2011*, Washington, DC, November 15, 2012, http://www.cbo.gov/sites/default/files/cbofiles/attachments/s1910.pdf.

[89] Ibid., p. 1. The estimates include costs associated with extending benefits to employees of the U.S. Postal Service, which is usually considered "off-budget," or outside of the normal federal budget process. Costs for extending same-sex partner benefits to USPS employees was estimated at $68 million from 2013 to 2022.

This estimate was $159 million and $211 million less than CBO's score of two similar bills from the 111th Congress (H.R. 2517 and S. 1102, respectively).[90]

CBO's score of S. 1910 assumed less than 1% of the federal employee and annuitant population would opt to enroll a same-sex partner in federal benefits programs. The score also estimated that federal government premiums for federal health care would be reduced by $13 million over ten years if same-sex partners were eligible to enroll. The savings would emerge, according to CBO, because the law would require health care providers "recover payments when a third party is liable for the health care costs of a covered enrollee" and such recoveries would reduce government premiums.[91] The CBO estimates of H.R. 2517 and S. 1102 from the 111th Congress did not include recovery payment collections in their analyses.

A 2008 academic study estimated the cost of extending same-sex partner benefits to federal employees *and* annuitants at $41 million in the first year and $675 million over 10 years.[92] In testimony before the House Oversight and Government Reform Committee's Subcommittee on the Federal Workforce, Postal Service, and District of Columbia on July 8, 2009, Office of Personnel Management Director Berry estimated that extending benefits to the same-sex partners of federal employees *and* annuitants would have cost the government $56 million in 2010.[93]

Current budgetary circumstances may discourage Congress from extending benefits to the same-sex partners of federal employees and annuitants. As noted earlier in this report, when DOMA was enacted, the House report that accompanied the legislation stated that a primary goal of the law was to "preserve scarce government resources."[94]

Congress often considers more than the cost or cost savings of a policy when choosing whether to act on it. Extending benefits to the same-sex partners of federal employees is controversial, and may prompt moral or ethical concerns for Members on all sides of the issue. Some Members, for example, may believe that extending benefits to the same-sex partners of federal employees violates a law enacted to require that marriage, for purposes of federal benefit programs, be defined as the union of one man and one woman. Other Members, however, may believe that

---

[90] Congressional Budget Office, *H.R. 2517 Domestic Partnership Benefits and Obligations Act of 2009*, December 17, 2009, p. 1, at http://www.cbo.gov/ftpdocs/108xx/doc10866/hr2517.pdf; and Congressional Budget Office, *S. 1102: Domestic Partner Benefits and Obligations Act of 2009*, Washington, DC, May 11, 2010, http://www.cbo.gov/sites/default/files/cbofiles/ftpdocs/114xx/doc11494/s1102.pdf. S. 1102 did not include extending benefits to the same-sex partners of federal annuitants, which H.R. 2517 did include. S. 1910 from the 112th Congress also included extension of benefits to the same-sex partners of federal annuitants. H.R. 2517 and S. 1102 included cost estimates to extend health insurance, survivor annuities, compensation for work-related injuries and travel and relocation benefits, which would have affected the federal budget. The bills sought to extend other benefits that would not have an affected the federal budget, such as life insurance and vision and dental benefits.

[91] Congressional Budget Office, *S. 1910: Domestic Partners Benefits and Obligations Act of 2011*, p. 3.

[92] Naomi Goldberg, Christopher Ramos, and M.V. Lee Badgett, *The Fiscal Impact of Extending Federal Benefits to Same-Sex Domestic Partners*, the Williams Institute, September 2008, p. 1. The study included cost estimates to extend health insurance, retirement benefits, travel and relocation expenses, family medical leave, long-term care, and worker death compensation, which would have an effect on the federal budget. The study also examined costs associated with vision and dental insurance, which would not have an effect on the federal budget.

[93] U.S. Congress, House Committee on Oversight and Government Reform, Subcommittee on Federal Workforce, Post Office, and the District of Columbia, *H.R. 2517, "The Domestic Partner Benefits and Obligations Act of 2009,"* 111th Cong., 1st sess., July 8, 2009, at http://www.opm.gov/News_Events/congress/testimony/111thCongress/07_08_2009.asp.

[94] U.S. Congress, House Committee on the Judiciary, *Defense of Marriage Act*, report to accompany H.R. 3396, 104th Cong., 2nd sess., July 9, 1996, H.Rept. 104-664 (Washington: GPO, 1996), p. 12.

---

prohibiting the extension of benefits to same-sex partners results in unequal treatment of federal employees in same-sex relationships. Still other Members may argue that extending benefits to federal employees in same-sex domestic partnerships is unfair to employees in opposite-sex partnerships. For example, at a House Committee on Oversight and Government Reform hearing in July 2009, Representative Chaffetz said the following:

> Whether or not a heterosexual couple is dating and living together can meet all other standards except for the portion ... regarding ... same-sex status is of concern to me. If they ... are not afforded the same rights, this bill is directly discriminatory against heterosexual couples, and that, to me, is one of the unintended consequences that I have a serious concern [about] and question.... [95]

This report, however, does not address the ethical and legal debates surrounding DOMA and same-sex marriage.

Policy Options and Specific Legislative Issues

Policy Options in Response to the Administration's Actions

As discussed earlier in this report, President Obama's June 2, 2010, memorandum to the heads of executive branch departments and agencies requires OPM to create and present to the President an annual report on agency progress toward the extension of certain benefits to same-sex domestic partners.[96] Congress may choose to stop the extension of these benefits by enacting legislation explicitly prohibiting their extension. No legislation has been introduced that would scale back the same-sex partner benefits extended by the Obama Administration. Conversely, Congress has the authority to enact into law some, all, or none of the memorandum. Congress may choose to hold hearings to examine the implementation of the memorandum.

Defining Same-Sex Partnerships

The definition of "domestic partner" is in dispute. DOMA defines marriage, for purposes of federal benefit programs, as the union of one man and one woman. For the purposes of distributing federal benefits to the partners of opposite-sex couples, the federal government recognizes a spouse from the date of legal marriage to either divorce or death. State and local governments or companies that wish to provide domestic partner benefits need to define "domestic partner" for the purpose of the benefits. Some state and local governments and companies that operate in jurisdictions that recognize same-sex marriage or domestic partnerships have required that same-sex partners be married in order to receive domestic partner benefits. Employees in states that do not recognize same-sex marriage would be required to meet the definition required by the entity that is providing the benefits. It may be difficult to define the

---

[95] U.S. Congress, House Committee on Oversight and Government Reform, Subcommittee on Federal Workforce, Post Office, and the District of Columbia, *H.R. 2517, Domestic Partnership Benefits and Obligations Act of 2009*, Hearing on H.R. 2517, 111th Cong., 1st sess., July 8, 2009, Serial no. 111-15 (Washington: GPO, 2009)

[96] The White House: Office of the Press Secretary, "Statement by the President on the Presidential Memorandum on Federal Benefits and Non-Discrimination, and Support of the Lieberman-Baldwin Benefits Legislation," press release, June 17, 2009, p. 3.

---

start and end of a same-sex partnership and because many same-sex partnerships are recognized in limited circumstances or not at all, the start and dissolution of such unions may vary based on jurisdiction. This could be problematic for the federal government as an employer because the federal government has employees in all 50 states, the District of Columbia, and the territories (as well as international employees)—some of which recognize same-sex marriages, some of which recognize domestic partnerships, and some of which do not recognize any same-sex partnership. If Congress chose to enact a law to extend same-sex partner benefits, it would have to define same-sex partnership to incorporate the various terms states use for such unions as well as capture such unions that exist in states that do not acknowledge same-sex relationships. In addition, Congress would have to specify what would constitute the start of such a partnership and what would qualify as its end.

Verifying Who Qualifies for Benefits

Married couples can use a marriage license to verify their committed relationship for legal purposes. Same-sex couples, however, have no license or other type of document to verify their relationship for federal legal purposes.[97] If Congress were to provide benefits to the same-sex partners of federal employees, Congress may also decide that the federal government must verify that benefit applicants are in a committed, same-sex domestic partnership.[98] Congress may determine that each agency should be given authority to verify whether an employee is in a same-sex relationship or if verification of a committed same-sex relationship would be more effective if it were centralized within OPM. Congress may choose to enact legislation that would make OPM the central clearinghouse for affidavits required to qualify for same-sex partner benefits. Designating OPM as the only agency with the authority to maintain those records could increase employee privacy, making it less likely that federal employees' private information is made public. Giving each individual agency the authority to maintain the affidavits could make the documents more susceptible to information leaks, as each agency could have a different system of recordkeeping. In addition, giving individual agencies the authority to file the affidavits makes it more likely that federal employees applying for the benefits may know the person with whom they must file the record, making the process less anonymous.[99] Some federal employees may be less likely to enroll in the program if they must identify themselves as gay or lesbian in front of a co-worker. Moreover, many federal employees may leave one agency to take a temporary or permanent position in another. OPM may provide the most logical clearinghouse for benefits processing because it could remove the need for employees who move from one agency to another to reapply for the same benefits. On the other hand, Congress may determine that OPM's mission does not include this type of government-wide recordkeeping role related to federal benefits. Giving individual agencies the authority to certify employee affidavits would not task OPM with a responsibility it may not have the capacity to undertake. Some have expressed the concerns about the potential for abuse and that some employees may claim to be in a partnership

---

[97] A state or local government-issued marriage license would not qualify for federal legal purposes because DOMA prohibits federal recognition of same-sex marriages.

[98] In most cases, agencies do not require a federal employee to provide the original or a copy of the marriage license to qualify for the extension of benefits to a spouse. Both bills in the 112th Congress that seek to extend benefits to same-sex partners of federal employees, however, would require the federal employee to sign an affidavit stating that he or she is in a "committed domestic-partnership." See H.R. 3485 and S. 1910.

[99] Agencies already administer the provision of certain benefits to spouses or same-sex partners, such as requests for sick leave or FMLA.

solely for the purpose of receiving benefits.[100] This could be the case if the requirements for obtaining recognition of a domestic partnership were less stringent than the requirements for opposite sex couples to obtain a marriage license.

Benefits for Domestic Partners

Some federal employees may not be married to their domestic partners, whether that partner is of the same or a different gender. As noted above, the domestic partners of these employees are not eligible to receive many federal benefits because they do not qualify as a "spouse," pursuant to federal law. In a House Oversight and Government Reform Committee report that accompanied a bill in the 111th Congress that sought to extend same-sex partner benefits, the committee wrote the following:

> federal employees living with opposite sex domestic partners have the option of marriage, which would entitle the employee and his or her spouse to the receipt of these benefits. Same sex partners may only get married in a handful of states. Even in these cases, the federal government does not recognize the marriage because of the Defense of Marriage Act (DOMA). H.R. 2517 does not affect DOMA. Therefore, under current OPM guidelines, same sex partners, even where married, are ineligible to receive these benefits as spousal benefits.[101]

Congress may choose to extend benefits only to those in legally recognized same-sex domestic partnerships. This limitation would control the costs associated with extending partner benefits by restricting the number of possible beneficiaries. Congress, however, may also consider extending benefits to the domestic partner of any federal employee, regardless of that partner's gender. Such action may attract more candidates to federal jobs. Such action also would permit an employee to qualify for federal benefits without having to identify the gender of his or her domestic-partner. Some employees may be hesitant to identify the gender of their domestic partner, even if the affidavit is confidential. The extension of benefits to such partners regardless of gender, however, could increase the costs of the FEHBP.

Taxation of Benefits[102]

DOMA precludes same-sex partners from being recognized as a married couple under the Internal Revenue Code (IRC).[103] A complete overview and analysis of the tax implications of same-sex marriage is beyond the scope of this report. However, the tax treatment of health benefits may be

---

[100] See, for example, the testimony of the Deputy Director of OPM at a hearing of the Senate Committee on Homeland Security and Governmental Affairs. See U.S. Congress, Senate Committee on Homeland Security and Governmental Affairs, *Domestic Partner Benefits for Federal Employees: Fair Policy and Good Business*, 110th Cong., 2nd sess., September 24, 2008, S. Hrg. 110-944 (Washington: GPO, 2008).

[101] H.Rept. 111-400, Part 1, p. 26 (footnote 6).

[102] This section of the report was written by Margot L. Crandall-Hollick, Analyst in Public Finance.

[103] Generally, the IRS does not recognize same sex couples as married. The IRS has ruled however, that starting in 2010 same sex couples living in states that recognize domestic partnerships and have community property laws (California, Nevada, and Washington), may combine their incomes and divide them equally, but still file as single or head of household. This may result in a reduction in the couple's overall tax liability if they would have been subject to a marriage penalty. In practice, some same sex couples have had difficulty complying with this ruling. For more information, see Laura Saunders, "Same-Sex Couples and the Marriage Penalty," *The Wall Street Journal*, February 19, 2011, and Scott James, "From I.R.S. to Gay Couples, Headaches and Expenses," *The New York Times*, June 11, 2011.

relevant to federal employees who are in same-sex relationships, particularly when one member of the couple works in the private sector.

Same-sex couples have a larger tax liability when one partner's health insurance benefits are extended to the other partner. While a federal employee's health plan cannot cover a same-sex partner, certain employers in the private sector choose to extend health insurance coverage to same-sex partners. The extension of this benefit often increases the tax liability of a same-sex couple. Under current law, opposite-sex spouses can exclude from gross income employer contributions to their health insurance plans. As a result of DOMA, same-sex couples must pay taxes on the employer contributions that cover a same-sex partner, sometimes referred to as "imputed income." For example, if an employer contributed $80 per paycheck to the cost of an employee's health insurance plan that covered a same sex partner, the employee would have to include some portion of the $80 in their gross income, increasing their taxable income (including payroll taxes) and ultimately their tax liability.[104]

In addition, if federal health benefits were extended to same-sex couples, but DOMA was not repealed, federal employees who extended their health coverage to their same-sex partner would also be subject to additional taxation from the "imputed income," as defined above.

Author Contact Information

Wendy Ginsberg
Analyst in American National Government
wginsberg@crs.loc.gov, 7-3933

John J. Topoleski
Analyst in Income Security
jtopoleski@crs.loc.gov, 7-2290

Acknowledgments

Alison M. Smith, legislative attorney, contributed to this report.

---

[104] Some employers have chosen to compensate same sex employees for the additional tax liability that occurs when health benefits are extended to a same sex partner. This policy is called "grossing up." For more information, see Tara Siegel Bernard, "For Gay Employees, an Equalizer," *The New York Times*, May 20, 2011.